Deadly

Hylas Publishing

First published in 2004 by Hylas Publishing
129 Main Street, Irvington, New York, 10533

Publisher: Sean Moore
Creative Director: Karen Prince
Art Director: Gus Yoo
Editorial Director: Gail Greiner
Editor: Sarah Postle
Designer: Sarah Postle
Illustrator: Adam J. Raiti

First American Edition published in 2004.
02 03 04 05 10 9 8 7 6 5 4 3 2 1

Library of Congress data available upon request.

ISBN: 1-59258-110-2

Set in Caslon and Clarendon

Printed and bound in the United States.
Distributed in the United States by National Book Network.
Distributed in Canada by Kate Walker & Company, Ltd.

www.hylaspublishing.com

Deadly

Phil Scott and Peter Engelman

To our parents, who always told
us to be careful…

Table of Contents

Human Errors

Here, There, and Everywhere

Follow the Yellow Brick Road

What Makes Us Go

War: What Is It Good For?

Hearth, Home, and Headstone

The Stuff We Couldn't Categorize

Deadly:
An Introduction

The world is one big deadly place.

In the good ol' days, people had to work hard to stay alive—foraging for food and shelter while worrying about being torn apart by saber-toothed tigers. The lifespan for the preponderance of human existence was 10 years. And so, we've spent the last few thousand years using our intelligence to figure out how to make life better, or at least, less deadly.

Although that toothy tiger is no longer a threat, Mother Nature and Chance still get in their licks. We live longer, have a wider variety of experiences, and, consequently, have a whole new bunch of deadly things to fear. We have to worry about being torn apart in an airline crash or dying from some malady rained down from surplus Cold War rockets. That's progress.

But, whether to the bathroom or the grave, we all gotta go sometime. We once ran into David Byrne (formerly of the Talking Heads), at an Army-Navy surplus store in New York City, buying a manual on building booby traps. We're always expecting to hear that one of his former bandmates has been found at Byrne's doorstep with a spring-loaded spike through his brain.

So, just how might we go? What are the deadly things? We've tried to identify a few of them in this book. All of the old favorites are here—airplane wrecks, car accidents, and natural disasters—along with some unusual bits—floods of molasses and death by barbecue grill.

Death, in any case, is everyone's topic. Death has an allure to which everyone can relate, and *Deadly* is everyone's book. *Deadly* transcends national boundaries and generational differences. We all fear death and occasionally must laugh at it. It's how we cope.

The content of *Deadly* is not something that we merely watch or read about. No, it is real things happening to real people. Anyone can get eaten by a dog or become one of the nearly half of all humans ever born who have been struck down by insects.

The book makes all of us interesting, as we live vicariously through someone else's peril. After all, someday, we will all succumb to a deadly thing.

Can you believe there are more than 110 million land mines estimated to be buried here and there all over the world? You should know where—exactly—the most are buried.

Deadliest man? Hitler, surely. Well, no. Stalin? Again, no. Chairman Mao? Right? Nope. Try the unknown man in Cortez's army, who delivered the smallpox virus to an unsuspecting South America. It was the gift that kept on giving.

We no longer spend all of our time trying to stay alive, and we instinctively miss that danger. So we try to recreate it through extreme games and reality television. The fear of death brings anxiety and adrenaline—the new drugs of choice.

But somewhere, in the back of our minds, we know that one day we will confront that deadly thing—and lose. Or we try harder still to avoid it.

The appeal of *Deadly* is that same intangible draw that makes you slow down to rubberneck at an accident. *Deadly* helps you do just that in the comfort of your own home. (So long as you stay away from the staircase...and you don't have one of those halogen lamps, do you?)

Reading this book is like junk food for the brain. When you're scarfing down potato chips, sometimes you think you just want a few, and you end up eating the whole bag. (By the way, that's really bad for you too.) But the lesson of this book—if there is a lesson—is to enjoy what time you have left. And think twice before booking that vacation in Algeria. Anyway, good luck. You're going to need it.

—Phil Scott and Peter Engelman

Unnatural Disasters

Good to the Last Drip

The Most Poisonous Plants

Ever since Socrates took his last sip, hemlock has been the big name in toxic plants. Just don't tell that to South American Indians.

While hunting for food, they like to dip their arrows in the juice of the *Chondrodendron tomentosum*, aka curare. "It's extremely fast and very deadly," says Brian Boom, vice president of botanical science for the New York Botanical Garden. Curare works by relaxing the muscles and inducing asphyxiation—an arrow so dipped will paralyze its victim in a matter of seconds, Boom adds.

Though no one has used it to knock off any pushy philosophers, a derivative called tubocurare is now used as an anesthetic to relax the heart muscle during open-heart surgery. "Scientists like to look at toxic plants to find new drugs," Boom says.

But how did the natives discover it was so deadly? "People will put something in their mouths, and if it makes them feel good, they keep doing it, and if they die, they find out that it's poisonous." Sorry about the discovery of curare, guys, but thanks a lot for peyote.

Mortal Thoughts
The world is a beautiful place
to be born into
if you don't mind some people dying
all the time
or maybe only starving
some of the time
which isn't half so bad
if it isn't you.

—Laurence Ferlinghetti
Poet and co-founder of City Lights Publishing

Passing Gas

A Very Dangerous Odor

 Rotting manure may stink, but there's another good reason to hold your breath. It produces hydrogen sulfide (H_2S), and a couple of deep breaths—containing around 600 parts per million—can cause you to lose consciousness. Continued inhalation will cause you to lose your life. No wonder so many kids are dying to leave the farm.

Mortal Thoughts
The trouble with quotes about death is that 99.999 percent of them are made by people who are still alive.

—Joshua Bruns
Author of *In Death*

CO Too

A Mass-Murderous Gas

No poison is more readily available than carbon monoxide. According to David G. Penney, Ph.D., professor of physiology at Wayne State University in Detroit, Michigan, and CO toxicologist of more than 30 years, 1,500 people die accidentally from inhaling carbon monoxide, and another 2,300 use it to commit suicide each year in the U.S.

"CO kills more people by far than any other poison in our environment," he says. "Its charm as a death gas relies on its accessibility—a by-product of solid, liquid or gas fuels, carbon monoxide is literally pouring out of the exhaust pipe of any running car."

Mortal Thoughts
Most people would rather die than think: many do.

—Bertrand Russell
Mathematician and philosopher who did not commit suicide as an adolescent because he wanted to learn more math.

A Little Dab'll Do Ya

The Most Lethal Neurotoxins

 Dr. Penney (see page 23) and other toxicologists agree that as far as toxicity, the deadly carbon monoxide gas has nothing on botulism, the most toxic substance found in nature.

Distributed widely in the great outdoors, botulism can be found in fields and streams and in the intestinal tracts of fish and mammals. Undercooked food is the most common culprit in the 30 or so cases that hit the U.S. each year. Botulism is a neurotoxin that causes respiratory failure, ultimately leading to death by asphyxiation within days if unrecognized or left untreated. It's so toxic that ingesting just a few billionths of a gram is enough to put you 6 feet under. However, over the past 50 years, the mortality rate of botulism has fallen from about 50 percent to 8 percent.

By comparison, the nerve gas sarin requires a much heavier dose of 0.5 thousandths of a gram to be lethal. But sarin's no toxic lightweight, either—it's 26 times more deadly than cyanide gas, used in the Nazi death camps during World War II.

That's not to mention ricin, which is 200 times more deadly than cyanide. If it's inhaled or ingested, just one milligram can kill an adult. Inhaled, it causes respiratory failure in 36 to 48 hours. Ingested ricin immediately kills the muscles and lymph nodes in the immediate area, followed by nausea, vomiting, and bleeding in the digestive tract and failure of the liver, spleen, and kidneys. The victim then dies from the collapse of the circulatory system.

Then there's VX, a nerve agent so deadly that a drop the size of George Washington's eye on a quarter (not Mount Rushmore) could kill a healthy man. In 2004, the Newport Chemical Depot began "chemically neutralizing" 1,269 tons of VX. Hmmm...1,269 tons. George Bush didn't have to go all the way to Iraq to find a weapon of mass destruction.

Mean Mother Nature

The Deadliest Natural Disasters

Here are the world's 5 worst natural disasters, according to David Crossley, chair and professor of geophysics at St. Louis University.

5. In 1737, 300,000 people were killed in Calcutta, India, by what was thought to be an earthquake. But plate tectonics rule that out—now everyone thinks it was a typhoon.

4. Shaanzi, China, was struck by a devastating earthquake in 1556. Since Richter hadn't been born yet, there is no known recorded magnitude. Nevertheless, more than 830,000 people died.

3. Ever wonder where the lost city of Atlantis really is? According to Plato, it was on the island of Santorini, which is all that remains of a volcanic explosion that occurred in 1500 BC. The eruption and the ensuing tsunami wiped out the Minoan civilization.

2. As for Noah's biblical flood, it actually could have happened around 3000 BC. At that time a global "paleoclimate event" occurred, which, according to Crossley, drastically altered the sea levels. It killed everybody, according to the Old Testament. Except Noah and his family, of course. Oh, and all those animals.

1. And the world's worst natural disaster (so far): an asteroid strike that occurred 65 million years ago, wiping out the dinosaurs and thousands of other species and giving rise to the age of mammals and ultimately, humans. Now, *that's* a disaster.

Heads Up

Way-Too-Close-to-Earth Objects

 Don't have enough to worry about? Nearly every month we hear reports about some asteroid on a collision course with the home planet, or that one whizzed close by without anyone noticing.

How about this? An asteroid 100-feet wide narrowly dodged the earth by 26,500 miles in March of 2004. That could have been a nasty day. One estimated to be about that size obliterated thousands of acres of forest in Siberia in 1908, and a really big one killed all the dinosaurs 65 million years ago (see page 27).

Too close for comfort? Fear not, NASA—the group that brought us Velcro, moon rocks and space junk—is keeping an eye on these "near earth objects" through its aptly titled "Near Earth Object Observation Program."

Apparently, a decent-size asteroid can kick up some pretty incredible damage, whether it hits land or causes a massive tsunami at sea. Not that NASA can do anything about it.

Can't wait for the real thing? Try this: (http://www.lpl.arizona.edu/impacteffects.) The University of Arizona's Earth Impact Effects Web site allows you to choose the size, speed, and density of your very own projectile at the location of your choice. It provides the results in the form of energy and thermal radiation created, impact crater size, fireball size, seismic effects, and ejecta—the amount of material thrown from the crater on impact.

Mortal Thoughts
Those who die seldom or never live to tell about it.

—Woody Allen
Famous neurotic

On Top of Old Smokey

Killer Volcanoes

 So you think you've got a temper? It's unlikely you compare to volcanoes, which really blow their tops. If you're volcano-phobic, you should avoid Indonesia—the country that accounts for two-thirds of all volcano-related deaths.

Top Five Eruptions

1. Tambora, Indonesia, in 1815—92,000 died of starvation.
2. Krakatau, Indonesia, in 1883—36,417 died from the resulting tsunami.
3. Mt. Pelee, Martinique, in 1902—29,025 died from ash-related disasters (roofs collapsing, air pollution, etc.).
4. Ruiz, Colombia, in 1985—25,000 died in mudflows.
5. Unzen, Japan, in 1792—14,300 died from the volcanic avalanche and resulting tsunami.

Slender is the Blight

The World's Worst Famines

Two famines stand out as the worst in modern times. The first was the Irish potato famine (1846 to 1850). The blight, which traveled from Mexico to the U.S. and finally reached Ireland in 1845, turned potatoes into black mush. Since potatoes were a staple for the 8 million Irish, more than 1 million starved and another million emigrated to the U.S.

That barely holds a candle to the seven million peasants who died in the Ukrainian famine. In 1932, Joseph Stalin raised Ukraine's grain procurement quotas by 44 percent, which was way more than the peasants could grow (if they wanted to feed themselves at the same time). Soviet officials confiscated seed grain, and anyone who didn't appear to be starving was executed on the suspicion of hoarding grain. Now there's incentive to stay on that vodka diet.

The Wild Kingdom

Sweat the Small Stuff

The Most Virulent Viruses

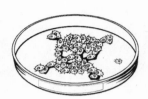

Bad things come in small packages. Until the early '70s, full-blown rabies—a virus that attacks the central nervous system and is usually transmitted through the saliva of wild animals—killed everyone who contracted it. Now, because of Fido's vaccines and immediate treatment options, the virus has become less lethal.

Of the 30 fun new viruses to emerge from the jungle in the last quarter-century, the one to avoid is ebola, which has a mortality rate of approximately 80 percent. Ebola turns your internal organs into bloody mush before it kills you.

Lucky for humans, it's not as easily transmitted as smallpox, whose most potent strain has a mortality rate of 30 percent (and though survivors are immune, the virus leaves pock-marks on its victims). The world's last major outbreak, between the 17th and

18th centuries, killed an estimated 60 million, (6.5 percent of the world's population) starting in the North American colonies, before Edward Jenner invented inoculation.

The last reported smallpox death was in 1977 and then the disease was pronounced DOA. We've even stopped the inoculations.

Today the only samples of the live smallpox virus exist in the U.S. at the Centers for Disease Control and Prevention (CDC) in Atlanta, Georgia, and in a poorly guarded building in Moscow. If some evil genius could get their hands on that Russian stash...well, let's not give them any new ideas.

Gesundheit

The Most Potent Plagues

As for other deadly microbes, a strain of the influenza virus turned especially virulent in 1918, killing nearly 22 million people worldwide—1.4 percent of Earth's citizens. That's more fatalities than World War I.

Before the advent of penicillin, the pneumonic plague—usually carried by rats—had a mortality rate of 99.99 percent. (But the good thing about the plague is, like smallpox, if you're lucky enough not to die the first time you get it, you're immune.)

The plague's finest hour, the infamous Black Death of 1347–51, killed at least 75 million people—between one-third and one-half of the world's population. Also known as the bubonic plague, it originated in China and quickly spread by merchant ships to Italy. Within months it engulfed Europe as far north as England.

So get your flu shots now, kids, and stop playing with dead rodents.

The Snake Man

Pets to Avoid

 After spending a record 7 days in 1998 locked in a room filled with poisonous snakes, Boonreung Bauchan, aka "the Snake Man," died in March 2004 after being bitten on the elbow by a deadly black mamba. His father donated Bauchan's box of pet serpents to the local zoo in Sri Saket, Thailand. Booreung would have wanted it that way.

Biting is not the only thing you have to worry about when it comes to serpents. The reticulated python can swallow a man whole, so it probably wouldn't make a good pet.

It's a Stain Killer, Too

The Planet's Deadliest Snakes

 Every year, as many as 80,000 people die from snakes bites—approximately 4 percent of the 1 to 2 million reported snake-bite "instances" worldwide.

Of the 8,000 people bitten by snakes each year in the U.S., only 9 to 15 actually die. In fact, most of the world's 450 "deadly" species of snakes can't live up to their name—they aren't big enough to bite a human, they can't deliver a lethal dose of their potent venom, or they're just too peaceful to give a damn.

One snake that can, according to Ken Kardong, a biologist at Washington State University, is Australia's tiger snake, which is big enough, toxic enough, and just about as pissed off as a reptile can be. But as far as venom lethality goes, the poor tiger snake ranks 14th. The snake with the most toxic venom is the hook-nosed seasnake, which can be found in a band stretching from the Persian Gulf to Northern Australia. It is followed by Russell's viper of southern Asia and the inland taipan of Australia.

Ironically, while Australia is home to the world's most toxic snakes (experts say that in the land down under, it's best to assume that any snake you step on is venomous), Sri Lanka holds the record for annual snake-bite deaths, with 800 reported fatalities in 1978.

On the bright side, snake venom can actually remove those stubborn blood stains from your laundry. Blood-stained jeans treated with an enzyme isolated from the venom of the Florida cottonmouth came out cleaner than untreated jeans, according to the American Chemical Society. According to scientists, the enzyme helps snake venom spread through the body by preventing blood from clotting.

Now here's a fun fact: Venom is injected, poison is ingested.

The Bugs and the Bees

The Deadliest Insects

Discounting casualties of war and accidents, the World Health Organization (WHO) estimates that the malaria-carrying anopheles mosquito has killed 50 percent of all people since the human race began about 3 million years ago.

In America, however, the deadliest insect is the common bee. According to Aetna's InteliHealth Web site (www.intelihealth.com), because of allergic reactions, each year bees take out an average of 100 people.

Mortal Thoughts
Our Constitution is in actual operation; everything appears to promise that it will last; but in this world nothing is certain but death and taxes.

—Ben Franklin
American statesman and printer

Bite the Big Apple

Getting bitten in New York City

Here's the number of people bitten in New York City in 1987, according to the International Shark Attack File. (Go figure: only 13 shark bites were logged that year, so you were more likely to be bitten by your deranged NYC uncle than by a shark.)

Biter	*Number of People Bitten*
1. Dogs	8,064
2. Other people	1,587
3. Cats	802
4. Rats	291
5. Squirrels	95
6. Raccoons	11
7. Ferrets	7
8. Skunks	3

Eight-Legged Frights

The Most Venomous Spider

 Try to avoid the Brazilian wandering spider. It's not only fast and aggressive, but it's also the most venomous spider in the western hemisphere. In other words, its bite kills. These 4- to 5-inch arachnids are also known as banana spiders, mainly because they've been found hiding on banana boats heading to the U.S. They grow pretty fast, too. So be sure and check your hat the next time you put on that Carmen Miranda outfit.

Mortal Thoughts

There is no terror in the bang, only in the anticipation of it.

    —Alfred Hitchcock
    Director noted for his cameo appearances

Fish Sticks

Underwater Poison

Here's one nasty critter—the reef stonefish, the most venomous fish in the world. Its 13 stout dorsal spines inject a highly toxic venom that causes intense pain. While no deaths have been recorded in Australia since the British convicts first arrived, reef stonefish probably killed many Pacific and Indian Ocean islanders.

People still get stung by the nasty devils every year; but luckily, scientists developed an antivenom in 1959. These venom carriers grow as long as 20 inches and look like a typical lump of coral. Hey, divers aren't supposed to pick up stuff anyway.

Shark Attacks

Who's Scared of Whom?

Damn, sharks are deadly. Well, maybe not all that deadly. The International Shark Attack File tells us that between 1580 and 2003, there were 1,909 confirmed shark attacks around the world (see list, page 45). Deaths numbered in the low hundreds. Just don't tell that to 8-year-old Jesse Arbogast, who survived having his arm bitten off by a 7-foot-long bull shark in the summer of 2001.

After Arbogast's uncle rescued the boy, he grabbed the shark and threw it up onto the beach. The shark died in a hail of gunfire, and the arm was recovered (and later reattached) after prying the mighty jaws open with a police baton.

We may lose the occasional battle, but we're winning the war; every year humans kill between 20 and 30 million sharks for everything from food to medicine to sport.

Shark Attacks Around the World

Region	Attacks	Deaths
United States	737	38
Australia	282	132
Africa	255	67
Asia	114	53
Europe	39	18
South America	89	21
Antilles, Bahamas	57	19
Bermuda	4	0
Mexico / Central America	57	31
Hawaii	96	14
Pacific Islands / Oceania	115	48
New Zealand	44	9
Other	20	6
Totals	1,909	456

Down Cujo!

The Most Dangerous Dogs

 According to a list compiled by Dr. Leslie Sinclair, DVM, director of veterinary issues for companion animals at the Humane Society of the United States, these 5 canine breeds have racked up the highest body counts:

Breed	Humans Killed (1979–1994)
1. Pit bull	57
2. Rottweiler	19
3. German Shepherd	17
4. Siberian Husky	12
5. Alaskan Malamute	12

So you're dying to say that the deadliest breed of dog, then, is the pit bull. Aren't you? Well, you would be wrong, says zoologist Dr. I. Lehr Brisbin of the University of Georgia.

During the early '80s, Brisbin was hired as an expert witness by a consortium of kennel clubs and breeders who successfully fought a ban on pit bulls. According to the good doctor, the true measure of a breed's deadliness isn't the total number of mangled bodies it brings to the back door, it's the number of bodies it produces compared with the total number of dogs in the breed. In other words, a breed with 50,000 dogs that kills only 1 person is deadlier than a breed with 250,000 dogs that kills 2 people. According to the doctor, the top 5 deadliest breeds would be:

Breed	Deaths per 10,000 dogs
1. Alaskan Malamute	8.84
2. Saint Bernard	7.8
3. Siberian Husky	5.96
4. Great Dane	4.82
5. German Shepherd	3.16

And so the now, relatively gentle pit bull comes in at a distant number 6, with 1.77 deaths per 10,000. Ah, the magic of statistics.

Get the Point

More Dangerous Dogs

 Brisbin's list (see page 46), however, does predate the surge in popularity of Rottweilers, so the maligned pit bull may even drop a notch to number 7. (Brisbin has no plans to update it.)

The ever-friendly golden retriever, by the way, was responsible for 1.66 deaths per 10,000 dogs, and Brisbin's research also turned up 1 death caused by a Dachshund. No, its owner didn't expire in a freak leash-tangling accident; the dog chewed the foot off an infant, who died from blood loss.

If there's a lesson here at all—besides how badly misunderstood those lovable pit bulls are—it's to avoid canines with the pointy ears. "Four of the first five deadly breeds are prick-eared, and three of the five are close to a wolf ancestry," Brisbin says. "This is probably why most all of the deaths are due to predation rather than aggression." Translating from "profspeak," Spot isn't mean, he's just looking for a meal like his distant wolf ancestors did.

Most dog victims are children and infants who are left alone with the animal, he adds, and to a dog, babies look like prey—they're small, they get around on 4 feet, they have high-pitched squeals that sound like a rabbit in pain, and they get scared and run when Spot growls and bares his fangs. And they taste like chicken.

Mortal Thoughts

On a large enough time line, the survival rate for everyone will drop to zero.

—Chuck Palahniuk
Author of *Fight Club*

Deer Me

Murderous Mammals

 Sure, man is the deadliest mammal, but guess what comes in at number 2?

Man-eating tiger? Rabid dog? Great white shark? Wait, that's not a mammal. Killer whale?

Nope, it's Bambi.

That's right, each year in the U.S. white-tailed deer kill an estimated 130 to 200 humans. Most of those deaths are deer-auto collisions, so the deer usually gets it, too.

The Animal Protection Institute reports that approximately 29,000 people are injured every year in deer-auto collisions, causing over a billion dollars in damage. And as many as 1 million deer bite the dust.

Deer are everywhere.

The Federal Aviation Administration recorded 420 deer-aircraft collisions in the '90s with more than $6 million in estimated damages. Presumably that's on the runway and not some airborne run-in with Santa and his flying deer.

Europeans are no safer. In their brief on reducing deer-auto collisions, professors Jochen Langbein, Rory Putnam, and Brian Staines note that approximately 300 people are killed and 30,000 are injured each year, in addition to the cool $1 billion in property damage sustained from cars hitting deer in Europe. And that doesn't even count all the damage they are doing to your garden.

Next most dangerous? Killer dogs come in a distant third, offing an annual average of 18 people. Some best friend.

Wildlife at 12 O'Clock

Airplane Enemies

This just in: The Wildlife Society bulletin has ranked the animals most dangerous to aviators.

First place, of course, goes to those deer again (see page 50). They're followed by flying types—vultures, geese, and even sparrows and swallows.

Birds and airplanes don't mix. In the U.S., between 1990 and 2003, approximately 60,000 bird-plane collisions were reported to the Federal Aviation Administration, though experts estimate that 4 times that were unreported.

What's the big deal? Wild animals—birds included—bounce off U.S. civil and military planes, causing $600 million in damage every year. And planes aren't the only things getting hurt. Since 1988, more than 195 passengers and crew worldwide have been killed because of collisions with wildlife.

According to the Bird Strike Committee USA, a 12-pound goose struck by an airplane traveling at a modest 150 miles per hour generates the force of a 1,000-pound weight dropped from a height of 10 feet. Imagine what that would do to your toes.

How do we know this? Engineers use what's called a Chicken Cannon to fire dead birds at test aircraft. (Hey, is that Chicken Cannon PETA approved?)

Airport-management types have come up with several ways to deal with these airport pests, most of which include firing loud, high-powered weapons as scare tactics. Blasting big guns around airplanes, though, means that the cure could be worse than the disease.

Human Errors

Master of His Domain?

The Deadliest Orgasm

A guy's first time can be scary, especially when he's alone. What's more, solo sex can also be deadly, especially when going after the aptly named "orgasm of death."

Each year, autoeroticism, a heightened orgasm reached through masturbation while choking off blood to the brain (usually with a rope or noose), claims an estimated 500 to 1,000 lives. Most victims are white teenage males.

Experts estimate that 25 percent of teen suicides are actually autoerotic attempts gone awry; embarrassed parents may have concealed such evidence as pornographic materials and sexual devices, or coroners may ignore or misinterpret the evidence.

Bend Over Frontward

Unsafe Sex

 If you're not really into the solo gig, you may still be able to experience auto-erotic asphyxiation. On the beat in Hong Kong harbor, Chinese prostitutes go head over heels for their clients. Floating out in the harbor on a boat, a prostitute leans forward and submerges her head. Her client—we'll call him John—will then penetrate her from behind.

As she reacts to her lack of oxygen, her body goes into self-preservation mode, which induces vaginal spasms. The spasms make the event far more pleasurable for John, who usually experiences a heightened orgasm before the prostitute pulls her head out of the water—just before she blacks out.

You'll probably want to practice in the bathtub before you go out onto the water.

That's a Blood Bath

The Most Dangerous Beauty Secret

 Sure, Vlad the Impaler gets all the headlines for being Bram Stoker's inspiration for *Dracula*, but more than a few scholars believe that Stoker's creation may have had a feminine influence as well.

With a motley crew of servants, Hungarian Countess Elisabeth Bathory (1560–1614) engineered the death of more than 600 women in order to bathe in their blood—her way of retaining her youth and vigor. She started out like most of us, killing small animals and then moving up to horses. But after slapping a servant bloody she felt that human blood made her more youthful.

Elisabeth drained the servant's blood into a vat and hopped right in. After that, there was no stopping her. At least not until she had killed some 612 girls in various manners; she hanged some from the ceiling for a bloody shower in her version of the Iron Maiden (called the "Iron Virgin").

Somehow the word got out that Elisabeth was up to something. In 1610, all the king's men—well, at least 1 of them, Count Thurzo—stormed the castle, executed the henchmen and imprisoned the countess for the last 3 ½ years of her life.

It seems that the count discovered a body in the basement—along with some of Elisabeth's future victims—and that put an end to the blood baths.

Mortal Thoughts
Ask her to wait a moment—I am almost done.

—Carl Friedrich Gauss
The mathematician's response, while working, after being informed that his wife was dying.

The Doctor Is In

The Deadliest Doctors

 Through the years, many men have been given or claimed the moniker Dr. Death. Here are but a few:

1. Dr. Harold Shipman. British mass murderer believed to have committed between 215 and 260 murders between 1975 and 1997. Most of his victims were elderly patients, though the youngest was 41.

2. Dr. Wouter Basson. Alleged apartheid war criminal accused of murdering hundreds of anti-apartheid prisoners to alleviate over-crowded prisons. The South African cardiologist also allegedly developed chemical and biological weapons for the white-minority regime during the '80s and '90s.

3. Dr. Jack Kevorkian. American euthanasia proponent who has helped more than 100 people commit suicide. He avoided criminal conviction for a decade, until 1998, when he single-handedly administered a lethal injection to a patient.

4. Dr. James Grigson. Forensic psychiatrist who says that murderers cannot be rehabilitated. He was an expert witness at over 100 capital murder trials in Texas over the past 40 years. His arguments were so compelling that the jurors chose the death sentence over something more lenient.

5. Philip Nitschke. Australian euthanasia proponent and founder of EXIT, an organization that distributes suicide devices like the Exit Bag, a plastic sack with a draw string for suffocation.

6. Gunther von Hagens. German physician who pioneered "plastination," in which corpses are impregnated with plastic and preserved for his traveling exhibits, "Body Worlds."

Drawn and Quartered

The Cruelest Punishment

Englishmen convicted of high treason were given a rather harsh sentence—they were hanged, drawn and quartered.

How is this done, you ask? Until 1870, the full sentence passed upon those convicted was as follows: "...you be drawn on a hurdle to the place of execution where you shall be hanged by the neck and being alive cut down, your privy members shall be cut off and your bowels taken out and burned before you, your head severed from your body and your body divided into four quarters to be disposed of at the King's pleasure."

To explain some of the archaic terminology, the convicted was tied to a sort of woven mat pulled along by a horse and "drawn" to the execution site. He was then hanged (without a drop so that his neck remained unbroken) and just before losing consciousness, he was cut down. Then, his penis and testicles were chopped off, his stomach was sliced open, and his intestines were pulled out and burned in front of his face. He was probably dead by then, though.

After that, his remaining organs were pulled out and his head was chopped off, his body was "quartered"—that is, cut into 4 pieces. This process may have also been accomplished using horses to pull the limbs in 4 different directions. The "quarters" were displayed on the city gates as a warning.

Women traitors got off pretty easy by comparison. For the sake of decency, they were merely burned at the stake.

Natural Born Killers

Human Exterminators

"Human"	Body Count
Adolph Hitler	35 million
Joseph Stalin	30 million
Mao Zedong	20–30 million

Then again, the deadliest person might not have been a power-mad 20th-century dictator at all, but rather, the unknown person in Hernan Cortez's 600-man raiding party, who was packing smallpox (see page 34) when they visited Mexico in 1519.

According to *Plagues and People* by William McNeill, the population of Native Americans was as high as 100 million at that time, including a total of 60 million in Mexico and Peru. Less than 50 years later, the disease had reduced the resistance-free populations to just 10 percent of their pre-Colombian levels. By 1620, the population of Mexico finally bottomed out at 1.6 million.

And a World War Too

The Deadliest Marksman

How many people can you kill with a couple of shots from a handgun?

Best case? Three? Four? Nine? How about 8.5 million deaths?

Credit 19-year-old Gavrilo Princip's 1914 assassination of Archduke Francis Ferdinand on the streets of Sarajevo as the spark that set off World War I, and you have the deadliest marksman in history.

The archduke's driver made a wrong turn and happened to back up the car right into the range of Princip, a member of the Black Hand society—a nationalist movement favoring a union between Bosnia-Herzegovina and Serbia. Princip fired into Ferdinand before unsuccessfully turning the gun on himself. He went to prison and died 5 years later of tuberculosis. Damn teenagers.

Here, There, and Everywhere

Vacation Stayaways

The Most Perilous Getaway

 Deadliest place in the world to visit? Florida.

That's according to an opinion poll of Europeans in the early '90s, when Florida's reputation took a big hit after several European tourists were murdered while visiting.

Mortal Thoughts
Famine. Check. Pestilence. Check. War. Check. Death. Check. And between the big events, the earthquakes and tidal waves, God's got me squeezed in for a cameo appearance. Then maybe in 30 years, or maybe next year, God's daily planner has me finished.

—Chuck Palahniuk
Author of *Fight Club*

Crime and Again

The Top Crime Countries

Nationmaster, a compiler of national and world data, reports that the U.S. easily has the most crime in the world, with almost 24 million incidents annually (counting assaults, robberies, murders, rape, capital punishment, etc.). The U.S. easily overtakes second-place Germany's 6 million annual episodes. But on a per-capita basis, Dominica takes the prize with almost 113 incidents per 1,000 people. The top 10 countries with the most total crime per capita in 2000:

Country	*Crimes per 1,000*
1. Dominica	113
2. New Zealand	108
3. Finland	102
4. Denmark	94
5. Chile	90
6. United Kingdom	86
7. Montserrat	83
8. United States	82
9. Netherlands	81
10. South Africa	80

Murder Capital USA

The Deadliest American Cities

Washington D.C. had 262 murders in 2002, according to the FBI. That's like killing 46 people per 100,000 residents—the highest rate in the U.S. for cities with a population over 500,000.

Rounding out the top 5 murder cities (per 100,000 residents) were perennial murder-capital-favorite Detroit, at 42; Baltimore, at 38; Memphis, at 25; and Chicago, taking fifth place with 22 murders. Los Angeles, however, racked up the most total killings that year—658. Still, that put La-la Land in ninth place on the per-capita list, with 17.5 murders per 100,000 residents.

Honorable mention goes to New Orleans, a city just under the 500,000 mark, for its 258 slayings—a robust rate of 53 victims per 100,000 residents. And that's why it's called the Big Easy.

Murder Nation

The Most Murderous Countries

The country that holds the record for the most murders, defined by Nationmaster.com as intentional homicide, is India with 37,170 in 1999. Coming in a distant second is Russia with 28,904 murders in 2000, followed closely by Colombia with 26,539, also in 2000.

On a per capita basis, however, Colombia takes top honors with 0.63 murders per 1000 people. South Africa comes in second on the per capita list (0.51 per 1000) and fourth on the total list (21,995) but claims the top spot as the country you are most likely to be murdered with a gun. Just another one of the things you'll never see in the travel brochure.

Mortal Thoughts
I'll moider da bum.

—Heavyweight boxer Tony Galento,
when asked what he thought of William Shakespeare.

71

Downtown

The Most Hazardous Cities

Deadliest city in the world? Algiers, the capital and largest city in Algeria, North Africa, rates lowest in the world in quality of life, public services, health care, and all-around social stability.

In Mexico City, the air pollution is so bad that they have emergency oxygen set up on street corners—much like the hilly North American cities that keep barrels of sand at roadsides to aid motorist's traction.

Mexico City also has a problem with rogue cab drivers, who are known to kidnap tourists—keeping them until their bank accounts are depleted and either dropping them in the boondocks or putting a bullet through their heads.

And Chernobyl (in the former U.S.S.R.) still has that ethereal glow from the meltdown of '86 (see page 132).

Despite all the obvious threats, says Robert Pelton, a travel writer specializing in dangerous places, the deadliest city could well be your own hometown. "Somebody who goes to Algiers is prepared for danger," he explains. "A lot worse things happen when you're not expecting it. You fly into a war zone, you go with a bulletproof jacket, and you're a lot safer there than chasing whores in Paris at three in the morning." So the lesson is: If you must go whore chasing, remember to bring along body armor.

Mortal Thoughts
I'm not afraid to die, I just don't want to be there when it happens.

—Woody Allen
American director, actor

Nation Hood

The Deadliest Countries

Human rights watchdog groups like Amnesty International and Human Rights Watch don't like to rank countries in the order of their hellishness—to them a government willing to snuff 30,000 of its own citizens is no worse than one that eradicates only 28,000. But most allow that if they did rank places, Colombia would rate somewhere near the top—at least in the western hemisphere.

Sure, things have calmed down a bit since 200,000 folks died in "La Violencia" between 1946 and 1958, but the South American nation's official war on drugs has turned into a 34-year-long civil war—politicians, journalists, businessmen, and the regular guy on the street have become targets for kidnapping and murder. According to Robert Pelton, author of *The World's Most Dangerous Places*, a sort of travel guide to lethal locales, some 18,000 were killed between 1990 and 1994, more than half of them civilians.

Every hour of every day someone is killed in Bogotá, the capital. The local health department lists "violence" as the leading cause of death for people over the age of 10. "If you go there, you will be the target of thieves, kidnappers, and murderers," Pelton says. The latest law is to ignore the law—it's now officially okay to not stop at a red light.

So many places, so cheap is life. There's eastern Turkey, where, according to travel writer Stephen Brewer, "The pro-government forces think you're a Kurd, and the Kurds think you're pro-government. Basically anyone out at night is fair game there."

Also, the Great Lakes region of east-central Africa has been a must-avoid place since 1994 when the Hutus and the Tutsi tribes began hacking away at each other with machetes.

Get a Bodyguard

A Wicked Place for Westerners

They don't cotton much to fereners over there in Algeria. Or, in the words of the U.S. government: "The U.S. Department of State urges American citizens not to go to or work in Algeria without substantial armed protection."

Few countries have a past as dark and disturbed; the North African country has been ensconced in violence since ancient times. More recently, the French managed to kill a quarter of a million folks there before pulling out in 1962.

Since the current government voided the results of its national elections in 1992, the radical fundamentalist Islamic opposition—and de facto winner—has murdered more than 13,000 civilians—targeting musicians, artists, journalists, and foreigners.

"It's the most dangerous place in the world for Westerners," says Robert Pelton, expert on world violence. "They don't care who you are in your mother country, they'll cut your throat. They're trying to prove that the government isn't in control."

If you must go (and Pelton went there a couple of years ago—without a bodyguard) he highly recommends that you avoid the Casbah and never stay in one place longer than 10 minutes, which is about how long it takes radical forces to get a gunman on you. And if you're an American and you insist on going out alone, the government will insist that you sign a disclaimer.

Mortal Thought
If somebody has a bad heart, they can plug this jack in at night as they go to bed, and it will monitor their heart throughout the night. And the next morning, when they wake up dead, there'll be a record.

—Mark S. Fowler
FCC Chairman

Here Today, Gone Today

Infant Mortality at Its Worst

 Life can be tough when you are young. According to the *CIA's 2003 World Factbook*, countries with the highest infant mortality rate are:

Countries	Deaths per 1000 live births
1. Mozambique	199.00
2. Angola	193.82
3. Sierra Leone	146.86
4. Afghanistan	142.48
5. Liberia	132.18
6. Niger	123.64
7. Somalia	120.34
8. Mali	119.20
9. Tajikistan	113.43
10. Guinea-Bissau	110.29

So who has the lowest infant mortality rate? Japan at a paltry 3.3 deaths per thousand.

That Seemed Old At 15

The Lowest Life Expectancy

The worldwide average life expectancy is 63.95 years, according to the *CIA's World Factbook.*

Countries with the shortest life expectancy from the *Factbook's* 2003 estimate include: Mozambique, 31.30 years; Botswana, 32.26 years; Zambia, 35.25 years; Lesotho, 36.94 years; Angola, 36.96 years; Malawi, 37.98 years; Zimbabwe, 39.01 years; Rwanda, 39.33 years; Swaziland, 39.47 years; and Ethiopia, 41.24 years.

Oddly, the world's richest nation, the U.S., came in at 77.14 years. That's 48 places behind longest-lived Andorra, the tiny mountainous region between Spain and France, which has an average life expectancy of 83.49 years. It's probably because there's no Andorran income tax—nor super-sized fast food.

Bargain Building

Construction Casualties

Forget the buildings where where the residents and workers become mysteriously ill (probably because of toxic chemicals used in their construction), or better yet, the buildings in big cities that pump in air from the traffic-polluted sludge found on the ground floor.

The deadliest building was a mall in Seoul, South Korea, that collapsed on June 30, 1995, killing 501 shoppers and injuring more than 900. The fire that followed burned for 2 days, but a few lucky Seouls managed to survive up to 16 days in the wreckage by drinking rain water. Shoddy design and construction were to blame. Nineteen South Koreans, most of them Seoul city officials, were convicted of negligence and bribery.

Beaten on the Beat

Not Quite Freedom of Press

The West Bank. Israeli Prime Minister Ariel Sharon used deadly force to dissuade journalists from reporting on its recent military incursion.

Colombia. In reprisals against the press by all factions in the civil conflict, 29 journalists have died there.

Afghanistan. Eight journalists were killed while reporting on the 2001 U.S. invasion.

Eritrea. This tiny African country has thrown at least 13 reporters in jail since 2000.

Belarus (of the former U.S.S.R). A local TV cameraman, Dmitry Zavadsky, disappeared on July 7, 2000. Though his body has yet to be found, 2 former members of the Belarusian special forces were convicted of kidnapping.

Iraq. Reporters Without Borders, a journalists' rights group, alleges that the pan-Arab TV station al Jazeera and the Palestine Hotel in Baghdad were fired on by U.S. military, killing 3 journalists and wounding 3 others.

Follow the
Yellow Brick Road

Unfriendly Skies

The Deadliest Domestic Airlines

The deadliest American carriers according to Airsafe.com (based on the number of accidents since 1970 with at least 1 fatality):

1. American Airlines/American Eagle, 12
2. United Airlines/United Express, 11
3. U.S. Airways/U.S. Airways Express, 9
4. Delta Airlines/Delta Express, 6
5. Continental Airlines/Continental Express, 5
6. Northwest Airlines/Northwest Airlink, 4
7. Alaska Airlines/Horizon Air, 3

Unfriendly World Skies

The World's Most Fatal Flights

The deadliest worldwide carriers according to Airsafe.com (based on the number of accidents since 1970 with at least 1 fatality):

1. Airlines of the former Soviet Union, 22
2. Air China and other airlines of the People's Republic of China, 17
3. American Airlines/American Eagle, 12 (tie)
3. Indian Airlines, 12 (tie)
5. United Airlines/United Express, 11
6. China Airlines (Taiwan), 10
7. US Airways/ US Airways Express, 9 (tie)
7. Turkish Airlines, 9 (tie)
9. Cubana, 8 (tie)
9. Garuda Indonesia Airlines, 8 (tie)

Runway Models

Airplanes Destined to Crash

The deadliest airliner is the Boeing 737, and its popularity is the reason.

It's the best-selling jet airliner in history, with more than 3,000 flying the friendly skies since 1968. And because they're used for short-haul flights, they make more takeoffs and landings—the most deadly part of any flight.

If that weren't bad enough, the only unsolved crashes in U.S. history (there are 2) occurred in 737s. Coming in second place, however, is its close relative, the Boeing 727.

Ignoring for the moment the thermonuclear hell that can rain down from a B-52H, which is capable of carrying 12 H-bombs, the deadliest military aircraft in history might be the McDonnell F-3 Demon.

Even before the first prototype left the ground, the U.S. Navy ordered the Demon in bulk to combat the Russkies' fierce little MiG-

15 in the early 1950's. The result—a severely underpowered aircraft whose engine tended to explode mid-flight.

Eleven accidents, many of which were fatal, happened within days after the beginning of the flight-test programs. The Navy grounded its Demons and ordered production to cease after fewer than 60 fighters had been built, costing taxpayers $200 million in 1955.

Mortal Thoughts
The loss of life will be irreplaceable.

—Dan Quayle
Former (thank God) U.S. Vice President

Riding on Fumes

Extremely Unhealthy Exhaust

A Partial List of Hard-to-Pronounce Hazardous Chemicals Found in Aircraft Exhaust:

1,1,1-Trichloroethane; 1,2,4-Trimethylbenzene; 1,3,5-Trimethylbenzene; 1,3-Butadiene; 1,4-Dioxane; 1,8-dinitropyrene; 1-methylnaphthalene; 1-nitropyrene; 2-methylnaphthalene; 3-nitrobenzanthrone.; 4-Ethyl Toulene; Acetaldehyde; Acetone; Acrolein; ammonia; Anthracene; Benzaldehyde; Benzene; Benzo(a)pyrene; Butane; Butyl Alcohol; carbon monoxide; Carbon Tetrachloride; cis-l,2-Dichloroethylene; Crotonaldehyde; Dichloromethane; Dimethyl Disulfide; Dimethylnaphthalene (isomers); Ethyl Alcohol; Ethylbenzene; Flouranthene; Formaldehyde;Freon 11; Freon 12; Heptane; Hexanaldehyde; Hexane; Isobutylaldehyde; Isopentane; Isopropyl Alcohol; m,p-Xylene; m-Cresol; Methyl Bromide; Methyl Ethyl Ketone; Methyl Isobutyl Ketone; Methyl

Phenyl Ketone; n,n-Dimethylacetamide; Naphthalene; n-Heptaldehyde; nitric acid; nitrites; nitrogen dioxide; nitrogen monoxide; nitrogen oxide; nitrogen trioxide; Octanal; Octane; o-dichlorobenzene; o-Xylene; ozone; particulate matter (PM10, PM2.5); Pentane; Phenanthrene; Phenol; Propinaldehyde; Pyrene; Styrene; sulfites; sulfur dioxide; sulfur oxides; sulfuric acid; Tetrachloroethene; Toluene; Trichloroethylene; urea; Veraldehyde; and finally, Vinyl Acetate.

While many chemicals in that list are known carcinogens, 3-nitrobenzanthrone may be the most hazardous compound ever to be tested for carcinogenicity. It scored substantially higher in the Ames toxicity test than its nearest rival, 1,8-dinitropyrene, also listed above.

How to Pick Your Seat

The Unluckiest Seat Assignment

 Here's something every frequent flier wants to know—where is the safest seat in an airplane?

In the back (the last part to reach the scene of the accident)? The exit row (you're first one out)? Over the wing (you're surrounded by way more structure)?

And the answer is...there is no answer. There are so many variations—the tail could strike first, the fuel in the wings could explode, the airplane could break apart at the exit rows—it's simply impossible to tell where the safest seat is until after the accident. So just sit back, and enjoy the ride.

Crash Landing

The Worst Wait for Rescue

In the off chance you've survived a ditching at sea, your worries aren't over. You still could become shark chum.

According to a report issued in early 2004 by *Flight Safety Digest*, you really want to be inside a life raft. Don't fish or clean fish, don't dangle anything in the water, and get rid of the dead—all those things bring on the sharks. But if you have to tread water, get rid of the brightly-colored life vest and any shiny, expensive jewelry, which attract the toothy beasts. Also, don't move around, remain in groups, try to not go poo-poo or pee-pee, and don't bleed. Now, if a shark grabs you, don't fight it—that's what prey do.

And hey, sharks aren't the only sea life that you'll attract. Watch out for Portuguese man-of-war, sting rays, electric rays, sea anemones, crocodiles, barracuda and venomous sea snakes. Now relax and wait for rescue.

Drive Me Crazy

Terrible Traffic

 You think flying is dangerous? It can't hold a candle to traffic. According to the World Health Organization (WHO), an estimated 1.2 million people die on the road each year, and around 50 million are injured. It's going to get worse, too. The WHO predicts that traffic deaths will reach 2.3 million people each year by 2020. Approximately 90 percent of those deaths will occur in underprivileged nations.

In 2002, 28 out of every 100,000 Africans died in auto crashes, compared to 14 out of every 100,000 in the United States.

The WHO and the World Bank also believe that the high death count is avoidable.

Stop drinking. Pay attention. Obey those traffic signs.

Drive Like Hell

Accident-Prone Automobiles

The 4 deadliest models of automobiles (fatalities per 10,000 cars), according to the Insurance Institute for Highway Safety:

1. Chevrolet Corvette, 4.7 fatalities
2. Chevrolet Camero (tie), 4.3 fatalities
2. Ford Mustang (tie), 4.3 fatalities
4. Pontiac Firebird, 3.2 fatalities

    Why these really fast, really fun cars? Well, they're usually not seen putting around Florida with the right turn signal blinking, are they?

Mortal Thoughts
Way I see it, we're all on the Hindenburg, no use fighting over a window seat.

    —Richard Jeni
    Comedian and frequent guest on the Tonight Show
    (Carson and Leno)

Road Weary

The Worst Country for Motorists

Imagine a country where 11 million new drivers hit the road each year without ever practicing on actual streets. Not to mention that those with connections just pay off the right person and get their license without any actual training.

It's a place where a question on the written test ponders whether you should return the vital organs of an unconscious driver to the body cavity from whence they came. No joke.

Traffic is like a scene from a Buster Keaton short—drivers battle for lanes, bikers joust for space (and presumably lose to the cars most of the time), signaling is virtually nonexistent, and motorists use freeway entrances for exits and vice versa. Yeah, we're talking China.

Overall, between 14 and 16 people are killed per 10,000 cars, compared with 1 person in Japan, about 2 in the United States, and 3 in France. Accidents with 10 fatalities have become commonplace, and 30 fatalities per wreck doesn't make the news. More than 300 people die every day, for an annual death rate in excess of 104,000. The head of the traffic bureau readily admits that more people die in traffic accidents here than in any country in the world. To think that private airplanes just became legal there.

Mortal Thoughts

Let us endeavor to live so that when we come to die even the undertaker will be sorry.

—Mark Twain
Reports of his death were greatly exaggerated.

Drive Below 85

The Deadliest Age for Drivers

Drivers over 85 are nearly 4 times as likely to die in a crash than middle-aged drivers, according to a study released by the AAA Foundation for Traffic Safety.

The study found that as drivers grew older, they suffered increasingly from decreased perception and motor skills. Frailty also caused serious injury and death in crashes that may not have killed younger people.

The study also found that the elderly are more likely to get into crashes while turning to the left, when drivers often must quickly question whether or not to stop. Drivers over 65 are 25 percent more likely to get in a crash than middle-aged drivers; drivers over 85 are 50 percent more likely to suffer a collision than middle-aged drivers.

Take the Bus

The Most Dangerous Driver

According to the *Guinness Book of World Records*, "a 75-year-old male driver received 10 traffic tickets, drove on the wrong side of the road 4 times, committed 4 hit-and-run offenses and caused 6 accidents, all within 20 minutes, in McKinney, Texas, on October 15, 1966." His name was not Mr. Magoo.

Mortal Thoughts

I have never killed a man, but I have read many obituaries with great pleasure.

—Clarence Darrow
U.S. lawyer and defender of monkeys at the Scopes monkey trial.

Parks for Not Parking

Nasty National Parks

Ahh, for the good ol' days of Yogi Bear harassing the heck out of poor Ranger Smith.

These days national parks have gone wild, and we're not talking about those wacky bears or adolescent party videos.

According to the U.S. Park Rangers Lodge 2003 survey, ill-equipped rangers are up to their necks in well-equipped drug smugglers, poachers, urban hoodlums, and illegal aliens. Some parks have all of those problems.

Organ Pipe Cactus National Monument, Arizona. It's a hotbed of smugglers, and by some estimates, 250 illegal aliens cross through the park each night. Shoot-outs with smugglers are common and a ranger was murdered in the summer of 2002 while investigating a drug deal gone bad. Four drug dealers were killed as well.

Amistad National Recreation Area, Texas. Another great place to smuggle, plus there's plenty of drugs and aliens, just like Organ Pipe. It shares 85 miles of the Mexican border, but has only 7 rangers. Oh, and their radio system is so old they don't make parts for it any more. Over.

Big Bend National Park, Texas. It has the longest boundary with Mexico, but management has ordered officers to stay away from the border if they suspect criminal activity and let aliens cross over. No use getting hurt.

Lake Mead National Recreation Area, Nevada/Arizona. Welcome to the only national park with its own armored car. No one's on duty at night, though, so it's open season for drunks and gangs. And even drunk gangs.

Coronado National Memorial, Arizona. What you get when you take a park and mix a small staff with drugs and smugglers.

Wheel of Misfortune

Death on the Road, Hollywood Style

Tom Mix. The silent-film cowboy was cruising fast along an Arizona highway in 1940 when he came upon a bridge under construction. He slammed on his brakes and a heavy suitcase tied on the back of his convertible came loose and shot forward into his head. He died almost instantly.

James Dean. In 1955, while driving his new Porsche Spyder to a race in Salinas, California, Dean smashed head-on into another car. His passenger was thrown clear and survived; the 24-year-old Dean died instantly.

Ernie Kovack. In 1962 his Corvair hit a utility pole in Los Angeles.

Jayne Mansfield. Blonde goddess Mansfield was on her way to an early morning talk show in New Orleans in 1967. Mansfield, her lawyer, Sam Brody, and her chauffeur, died when their speeding Cadillac plowed into the back of a slow-moving mosquito-spraying truck. Her 3 kids, all riding in the rear seat, survived.

Steve Allen. When famed comic Allen died in October 2000, in Encino, California, the first news reports attributed it to a heart attack. Later, an autopsy revealed that the cause was a hole in his heart known as a "hemopericardium." The day he died, someone backed an SUV into Steverino's car, which bruised his chest and ruptured his heart.

Mine Your Step

The Most Dangerous Places to Walk

 On the subject of land mines, exact figures are hard to come by—no one can seem to remember where they left the damn things.

But according to the Cooperative for Assistance and Relief Everywhere, Inc. (CARE), as many as 110 million mines are buried somewhere around the globe, and another 100 million are stockpiled.

Belligerent parties have been burying and forgetting them since World War I, and they tend to not go away until someone steps on them, which happens about once every 15 minutes. A total of 11,700 people, including 2,649 children, were reported killed by land mines in 2002, according to The International Campaign to Ban Landmines.

The country with the highest density of land mines is Bosnia-Herzegovina, with 152 mines per square mile.

But in the race for sheer numbers, B-H's 3 million mines comes in a distant eighth place. The top winners include:

1. Egypt   23 million mines
2. Iran   16 million mines
3. Angola   9–15 million mines

According to the United Nations, Iraq, China, Afghanistan, and Cambodia each have around 10 million land mines strewn about somewhere. After Bosnia, comes its friendly neighbor Croatia, with 2 million mines.

Norah Niland, a humanitarian affairs officer for the U.N., says the surprisingly high figure for Egypt is because its mines are left over from World War II and the '67 War, in which Israel attacked and defeated Egypt, Syria, and Jordon. "Egypt has taken the stance that they want the countries who laid them to come and remove them," she says. Good luck.

Overboard

Lots of Deadly Yachts

Natalie Wood. After spending Thanksgiving 1981 with hubby Robert Wagner and actor Christopher Walken on the yacht *Splendour*, Wood was found floating near Santa Catalina Island, California, on the morning of November 29, nearly a mile from the ship, wearing a dressing gown and a down jacket.

Robert Maxwell. When the media mogul's crew docked his yacht, *Lady Ghistlaine*, in Los Cristianos, the Canary Islands, Maxwell turned up missing. His naked body turned up floating 20 miles off Gran Canaria Island. Later, investigators found that his vast empire—including Maxwell Communications, the Mirror Newspaper Groups and Macmillan Publishing—was near financial collapse, supporting the theory that Maxwell committed suicide.

Joseph Pulitzer. With his yacht,

Lady Liberty, anchored off Charleston, South Carolina, in October 1911, the nearly blind newspaperman began having severe chest pains. He died not long after his family arrived from New York.

Thomas Ince. In 1924, the filmmaker was a weekend guest on William Randolph Hearst's yacht *Oneida*, along with Charlie Chaplin, columnist Louella Parsons and Hearst's main squeeze, Marion Davies. After allegedly suffering heart failure, Ince's body was removed from the yacht in San Diego and cremated. But a rumor persists that Ince made a pass at Davies, and a jealous Hearst shot him.

Dennis Wilson. The Beach Boys drummer was diving from the yacht *Emerald* off Marina del Rey, California, in 1983. Searching for some personal items that he'd tossed overboard earlier, Wilson apparently got tired and drowned. An autopsy revealed that he had been drinking.

Death Takes a Field Trip

Deadly (If They Were True)

The Conspiracy Museum
110 S. Market Street
Dallas, Texas 75202
214-741-3040
Admission: $7 for adults, $6
for seniors and students and
$3 for children 12 and under

A paranoid's trip through American history, the Conspiracy Museum offers a good grounding in conspiracies you may not have known existed.

There's the Lincoln assassination conspiracy, which maintains that John Wilkes Booth actually got away and implicates Vice President Andrew Johnson, who allegedly double-dated sisters with Booth.

And of course, the Kennedy assassination conspiracy, which alleges that the Mafia, the CIA, the Military-Industrial Complex, and the FBI all had hired guns all over that grassy knoll at Dealey Plaza (see Oliver Stone's movie *JFK* for further details).

Not to mention the Robert Kennedy assassination conspiracy—like his brother, RFK wanted to end the Vietnam war, (which would be bad for big business).

The Martin Luther King assassination conspiracy—also wanted to end the war, also bad for business.

The Ted Kennedy assassination conspiracy in which the conspirators snuffed Mary Jo Kopechne as a warning to Teddy to keep that war going.

And the KAL Flight 007 conspiracy, which was created to foster anti-communist sentiment in the U.S.

The Conspiracy Museum, located near Dealey Plaza, is an afternoon of fun for the whole family.

They've Cleaned Up

Axe-ident Prone

*Lizzie Borden Bed &
Breakfast
92 Second Street
Fall River, MA
508-675-7333*

More than a century after Lizzie Borden allegedly murdered parents Andrew and Abby Borden (August 4, 1892), the Greek Revival home has become a warm and cozy B&B. It offers a choice of 6 rooms, plus a breakfast much like that enjoyed by the Bordens on the morning of their date with fate: bananas, johnnycakes, sugar cookies, and coffee. And if you're too squeamish to spend the night, daytime tours are available. It's just 50 miles south of Boston, close to Cape Cod and Providence or Newport, Rhode Island, and it's near all major highways.

Island Paradise

Hazardous Health Research

Plum Island Animal Disease Center
Plum Island
9 miles off Old Saybrook, CT 06475

Ninety-two scientists research high-conse-
quence biological threats, such as foot-and-
mouth disease and high-volume contamina-
tion of food supplies, on this bucolic 840-acre
island paradise. Named for the native plum
trees that line its beaches, the center also
leads research to prevent, respond to and
recover from the intentional introduction of
animal diseases.

In a 2003 speech, Senator Hillary Clinton
(D-NY) called the island's security inadequate,
and charged that the USDA, which runs the
island, "behaved in a cavalier manner toward
the serious risks associated with the research
that is done at the facility." No tours available. Sorry.

What Makes Us Go

Pus in Boots

Poisonous Pimples

 More people die of acne in Mexico than any other country in the world. Okay, so its only 3 people annually but that's just another reason to wash your face, cut back on the chocolate, and quit touching yourself you-know-where. Denmark, Croatia, Germany, and Lithuania tie for second with a single acne death each, according to Nationmaster.com. No mention is made of the danger of facial acne versus the dreaded back acne.

Mortal Thoughts

Dying is easy. Comedy is hard.

—Last words of Edmond Kean
Legendary deceased English actor

How We Go

Risk Factors to Watch Out For

The World Health Organization (WHO) tracks "selected leading risk factors" that contribute to death worldwide and notes the number of fatalities caused by each. In 2000, the leading risk factors were:

1. Blood Pressure   7,200,000 deaths
2. Tobacco   4,900,000 deaths
3. Cholesterol   4,400,000 deaths
4. Underweight   3,700,000 deaths
5. Unsafe Sex   2,900,000 deaths
6. Insufficient Fruit and
   Vegetable intake   2,700,000 deaths
7. High Body Mass index   2,600,000 deaths
8. Physical Inactivity   1,900,000 deaths
9. Alcohol Consumption   1,800,000 deaths
10. Unsafe Water,
   Sanitation and Hygiene   1,700,000 deaths

Time to put out your butt, get off your butt, and for goodness sake wash your hands.

Fighting For Peace

Fatal Places for Peacekeepers

You think keeping the peace between your brother and sister is tough, how about doing it between warring nations? U.N. peacekeeping forces have endured 1,906 fatalities since their inception in 1948. India has lost more peacekeepers than any other country with 109 fatalities, followed by Canada (106) and Ghana (100).

There have been more fatalities since the Berlin Wall fell in late 1989 (1,080 fatalities) than during the Cold War (826 fatalities). Perhaps there was something about the threat of nuclear annihilation that made people stop killing each other.

Take a Deep Breath

Potent Pollution

According to the World Health Organization (WHO), 3 times as many people die from the effects of air pollution than are killed in traffic accidents. Deaths from air pollution are under appreciated; they lack the drama of a car wreck, which makes better headlines than someone succumbing to lung ailments and slowing dying over time. That's hardly a spectator sport.

Mortal Thoughts

Now, my good man, this is no time for making enemies.

—French philosopher Voltaire, on his deathbed, responding to a priest asking him to renounce Satan.

One More For the Road

Dangerous Dinner Drinks

In late 2003, French winemakers unveiled a response to all this pap about the dangers of drinking and driving. It seems that a crackdown on drunk driving had reduced wine sales at restaurants by about 15 percent. The winemakers felt the government was just overreacting, and launched a campaign to let drivers know they could have "two or three" glasses of wine and still be able to navigate safely. Further plans are to install Breathalyzers at restaurants so patrons can drink responsibly.

You'll need a drink after reading this: Forty percent of all accidental deaths involve alcohol.

You Gotta Go Sometime

The Deadliest Places Not to Pee

 Certainly one of the great tests of stamina is "holding it," but who knew you could die from urine retention? They keep stats on that sort of thing?

Indeed, Nationmaster.com tells us that more people in Egypt have died from urine retention than any other county. Would you believe 21 deaths? The Netherlands comes in second with 8 fatalities followed by a tie for third between Croatia and Ecuador with 3 each. But why Egypt? It's practically a huge litter box—just go, man.

Mortal Thoughts
Where are you going? A real man can hold his urine.

   —Cartoon from *National Lampoon Magazine*, mid '70s

Eat, Drink, and ...

Last Suppers

The Deadliest Dinners

Aside from a heaping plate of surf-n-turf—consisting of uncooked, E. coli-laced steak and unpasteurized, bacteria-riddled shellfish— the deadliest meal could well be a tiny helping of fugu.

Considered a delicacy by the Japanese, who are willing to fork over more than $400 for one meal, fugu is made from specially prepared puffer fish, whose liver, skin, intestines, and yes, gonads, contain the deadly poison tetrodotoxin. Tetrodotoxin has a mortality rate of 60 percent; each year some 50 Japanese unintentionally make fugu their last supper.

And speaking of last suppers, what are the favorite final meals on death row these days? According to Brian Price, author of *Meals to Die For*, inmates' favorite final meal leans toward cheeseburgers and french fries, though many request fried chicken, steak, and ice cream. Price, who served 14 years in

Huntsville Penitentiary for abduction and sexual assault, prepared 220 final meals as a cook in the prison kitchen. Most wanted meat and potatoes, though one requested chicken with fried squash and eggplant, mashed potatoes, snap peas, boiled cabbage, corn on the cob, spinach, and cheese-covered broccoli.

Until December 2003, the Texas Department of Criminal Justice listed every last meal death row inmates requested since 1982, when the state resumed capital punishment—313 meals in all. The department eliminated the list after receiving complaints that it was offensive.

Evil Vending Machines

Killer Snack Attacks

 Between 1978 and 1995, diabolical vending machines rose up, killing 37 people and injuring another 113. According to the Consumer Product Safety Commission, the victims were rocking or tilting the machines hoping to procure a free soda or maybe some change. Now vending machine manufacturers supply the machines with warning signs and, in case the tippers can't read, diagrams showing the machines falling over onto them.

Mortal Thoughts
The idea is to die young as late as possible.

—Ashley Montagu
Articulate but accessible Englishman

On the Road Again

The Most Dangerous Driving Eats

If you're among the 65 percent of Americans who like dining while driving, you should avoid the following foods—if you want to stay in one piece. In reverse order:

10. Chocolate. It drops. You want to clean it. You get distracted.

9. Soda. You spill it.

8. Jelly donuts. Drips on your nicest suit.

7. Fried chicken. Your hands get greasy and grip-less.

6. Barbecue. Sloppy.

5. Hamburgers. You can't keep the insides from spilling outside.

4. Chili. It's hot. You have to spoon it. Both hands become occupied.

3. Tacos. Just try to keep them together.

2. Hot soup. (See Chili above.)

1. Coffee. It's hot and you're sleepy. (Why else would you drink it?)

Acute Indigestion

Deadly Delicacies (For Some)

 Then there's a rare condition out there called "pica," whose sufferers eat things not quite in the food category (and not even tasty at that)—toothbrushes, dirt, burned matches, hair, soap, ashes, and chalk.

One patient blew doctors minds when they dicovered the cause of his sore and distended stomach. The 62-year-old man had chowed down $650 worth of coins, along with other metallic objects such as needles and necklaces. Surgeons successfully removed the 12-pound mass (which had pulled his stomach down to his hips) but the patient died 12 days later.

School Lunch Program

A Murderous Meal

You know the old school-lunch drill—the hamburgers from Monday are diced up and used to make the Tuesday meatloaf, which is then added to a broth to make Wednesday's vegetable beef soup, which mutates into Thursday's goulash. Friday they give up and throw you a hot dog (converted to hamburger for Monday).

As bad as that sounds, it doesn't even come close to the school lunch served up in the village of Taucamara, Peru, in October 1999. Someone inadvertently prepared powdered milk in a canister that had been used to mix strong insecticides. Twenty-four children died after eating the school lunch meal of bread and milk.

You won't complain about that meatloaf ever again.

Occupational Hazard

Sick of the Job

Career Casualties

 Each year in the U.S., there are a whopping 60,300 deaths from occupational diseases such as asbestosis, according to Jim Young, spokesperson for the New York Committee for Occupational Safety and Health.

One reason: Of the nearly 76,000 chemicals in commercial use, 71 percent lack minimal toxicity information, including screenings to determine if the substance is cancer-causing. In fact, the tip-off that a substance may be deadly to consumers is that the poor bastards who work with it start getting sick, adds Young.

Each day, more than 160 workers die in the U.S. alone. "The causes range from everything from falling from a high-rise under construction, to tractor accidents, to a long, slow death from cancer, to being murdered," he says. "People think murder's not job-related, but it is."

What are your chances of being murdered on the job? Ask yourself: a) Do I handle money? b) Do I work alone? c) Do I work in a seedy neighborhood? d) Have I pissed off any of my fellow U.S. Postal Service workers?

If you answered yes to a, b, and c, you're either a taxi driver or a convenience store clerk. Get a new job. If you answered yes to d, buy body armor and move.

Going on the Job

The Deadliest Work Day: Everyday

 More than 5,000 people die everyday on the job, according to the International Labor Organization (ILO). That's an annual worldwide death toll exceeding 2 million. And, depending on the occupation, there are 500 to 2,000 injuries for every death. The majority of those deaths are cancer (32 percent), followed by circulatory diseases (23 percent), and accidents (19 percent).

Even kids can become victims; 12,000 children die each year on the job. And we're not talking about little Johnny's paper route. The ILO estimates that 80 percent of job accidents are avoidable if people would just be more careful. That means, if you workers only tried harder, you wouldn't develop cancer.

Industrial Strength

The Worst Factory Failure

In the late '60s, Union Carbide began manufacturing sevin, a pesticide, in a plant in Bhopal, India, to capitalize on India's drive for agricultural independence. In 1979, the plant quit importing a key ingredient, methyl isocyanate (MIC), and began to manufacture it on-site.

On December 23, 1984, a chemical reaction started in a MIC storage tank as a result of the addition of a large amount of water. MIC began to leak into the air, and by the time the flow was stopped, 40 tons had been released. The results were devastating—thousands died in their sleep. The death toll is estimated at 4,000 and the effected population at nearly half a million. Negative health repercussions to the inhabitants continue nearly 20 years later.

Nuclear Threats

Radioactive Wrongdoings

In the early morning of March 28, 1979, an automated response generated in the non-nuclear area of the Three Mile Island reactor complex triggered a series of events.

A relief valve stuck open, allowing the release of too much water, which kept the reactor core covered. The resulting damage to the core and the workers inability to promptly decide on corrective action caused a release of about 2.5 million curies of radioactive gases and 15 curies of radiodines. This affected some 2 million people in the surrounding area. No one died as a direct result of the incident.

But that doesn't hold a glowing candle to what happened at the Chernobyl nuclear power plant, near Kiev, Russia. Careless operation during an "experiment" started an uncontrolled reaction that resulted in explosions and a fireball that blew the heavy steel and concrete crucible apart.

More than 30 people died as a result, and 135,000 residents were evacuated as a cloud of radioactive debris spread over most of Europe. Increased instances of thyroid and other cancers in the nearby inhabitants and another 2,500 deaths have been linked to the disaster.

In order to contain what was left of the accident, a massive "sarcophagus" was constructed using steel and concrete. Refinements on the sarcophagus are still in progress. An estimated 200,000 people were eventually relocated, and 4,000 square miles surrounding the area remain barren.

The Final Frontier

Spacecraft Disasters

Astronauts and cosmonauts killed:

1. January 27, 1967—Astronauts Gus Grissom, Edward H. White, and Roger B. Chaffee died when a fire swept through their *Apollo* command module during a ground test at Kennedy Space Center, Florida. The capsule was filled with 100-percent oxygen, which exploded following a spark caused by faulty wiring.

2. April 24, 1967—Soviet cosmonaut Vladimir Komarov died when his *Soyuz I* spacecraft crashed in Russia. The main parachute didn't deploy.

3. June 29, 1971—Thirty minutes before landing, Georgy Dobrovolsky, Vladislav Volkov, and Viktor Patsayev died when a faulty valve depressurized their *Soyuz 11* spacecraft. The cosmonauts weren't wearing their pressure suits at the time.

4. January 28, 1986—Just 73 seconds after liftoff, the space shuttle *Challenger* exploded, killing the 7 astronauts on board: Francis "Dick" Scobee, Michael J. Smith, Ellison S. Onizuka, Judith A. Resnik, Ronald E. McNair, Gregory B. Jarvis, and Christa McAuliffe (who was to be the first teacher in space). Flames shot through a stiff O-ring, which caused the joints in the solid fuel booster rocket not to seal, and ignited the liquid-fuel main tank.

5. February 1, 2003—Just 16 minutes before it was scheduled to land at Cape Canaveral, Florida, the shuttle *Columbia* disintegrated 200,000 feet above Texas. William McCool, Rick Husband, Michael Anderson, Kalpana Chawla, David Brown, Laurel Clark, and Ilan Ramon (who was Israel's first astronaut), died almost instantly. The investigation revealed that foam from the main fuel tank broke away during liftoff, busting a hole in the wing. On reentry, hot gas penetrated the wing's innards and the shuttle burned up.

A Sticky Situation

The Deadliest Sweetener

Around the turn of the 20th century, molasses was one of the world's most popular sweeteners. United States Alcohol, a molasses manufacturer, built a 52-foot-high tank with a 90-foot diameter in Boston, Massachusetts, to contain 2.3 million gallons of molasses.

Responding to reports that its huge tank was weak, United States Alcohol painted the container brown, the color of the sweetener, so the leaks would be less noticeable.

Unfortunately, the paint job didn't solve the problem.

On the morning of January 15, 1919, the vat heated up too quickly and exploded. Steel plates from the tank flew apart with such force that they toppled an elevated train and jarred buildings from their foundations (some even collapsed). The entire area, including the buildings, was slathered in the sticky goop. A fire station was put out of commission and 21 people lost their lives. Wow, that could never happen again. Or could it?

Sticky: Part II

More Murderous Molasses

 The town of Sucarnoochee, Mississippi, was a center of sugar refining in the early '30s, and had mechanized the work so that it could process 2 million gallons of molasses at a time. Just after lunch on December 11, 1932, a steam valve was mistakenly closed during production and moments later, ol' boiler number 2 exploded, wrecking the support scaffolding and dumping 2 million gallons of molten molasses right down Main Street. Fatalities? Twenty-one.

Not a community to mope about its misfortune, in the late '50s, the town decided to commemorate the event with the Sucarnoochee Molasses Disaster Festival, which includes a reenactment of the incident.

Each year, a group of hardy souls—many of them descendents of the original victims—try to keep ahead of 10,000 gallons of corn syrup poured down Main Street. And people say Boston is a fun town.

That's Entertainment

Audience Appreciation

The Deadliest Film for the Viewers

 On August 20, 1977, during a screening of the Iranian movie *The Deer*, in Abadan, Iran, arsonists torched the Cinema Rex theater, killing an estimated 422 movie-goers. The police force rounded up the usual suspects, members of a Muslim extremist group that opposed the Shah. Later reports surfaced claiming that the police barred the flaming theater's doors and fought off rescuers with clubs and machine guns.

Mortal Thoughts
He is one of those people who would be enormously improved by death.

 —H.H. Munro
 Author and political satirist

The Actors' Studio

The Deadliest Films for the Actors

The 1956 movie, *The Conqueror*, usually makes the critics' worst-films list (John Wayne as Genghis Khan—need we say more?), but the motion picture became doubly cursed by being shot near a nuclear test site in Utah. Many of the cast and crew later developed cancer, including Wayne, his on-screen love interest Susan Hayward, and Agnes Moorehead.

And how about the curse of *Rebel Without a Cause*? Stars James Dean, Sal Mineo, and Natalie Wood all died tragically, while supporting actor Jim Backus, as Thurston Howell, III, kept narrowly missing rescue from Gilligan's Island.

Mortal Thoughts

I want a priest, a rabbi, and a Protestant clergyman. I want to hedge my bets.

—Wilson Mizner
U.S. screenwriter and playwright

A Real Shoot 'em Up

The Deadliest Films for the Extras

If there's someone out there counting the number of bullet-riddled corpses littering the silver screen, we couldn't find him. But according to Jim Reynolds, chief researcher on the 3-year study (1994–97) on TV violence for the UCLA Center for Communication Policy, the most violent theatrical release shown on network television was *Under Siege*, a 1992 action thriller starring hammy Steven Seagal as a cook and pinup poster babe Erika Eleniak as a pinup poster babe.

According to the center's report, "The film contained more than 50 acts of violence, far more per hour than found in any series or television movie...We know of no way that this film could be edited sufficiently so that it could run without raising concerns for violence."

Of course, ABC did edit out the flick's sole redeeming scene—Eleniak baring her breasts. Without it, the movie was meaningless.

Brutal Bean Ball

The Most Murderous Pitch

 Raymond Johnson Chapman (1891–1920), Cleveland Indian's shortstop, died after a blow to the temple by a pitch from Yankee Carl Mays. The only player killed in a major-league baseball game, Chapman never regained consciousness, despite emergency surgery.

Mortal Thoughts
He'd have the best, and that was none
  too good;
No barrier could hold, before his terms.
He lies below, correct in cypress wood,
And entertains the most exclusive worms.

—Dorothy Parker
American author and satirist
A tombstone for *The Very Rich Man*

Hold on Tight

Killer Carnival Rides

Yeah, those carnival rides look dangerous. Hell, they are dangerous.

According to the U.S. Consumer Products Safety Commission, 4.4 people died on amusement rides each year between 1987 and 2001. The CPSC estimates that between 1997 and 2001 more than 6,500 people were injured each year on fixed-site amusement rides.

The most dangerous year? 1999, with an estimated 7,629 injuries. Over that same period, more than 2,700 people were injured annually on mobile amusement rides. More females died than males, and the most common fatalities were children between the ages of 5 and 14, caused by roller coasters.

As for mere injuries, almost 40 percent occurred in July and August. Females made up 60 percent, and one-third of all injuries happened in the 25 to 44 age group.

And the most accident-prone body part? Forty percent of injuries were to the shoulder/arm/hand complex, with the head/face/ear region placing a distant second at 20 percent.

The most common type of injuries were strains and sprains at just over a third, with contusions and abrasions placing second at 26 percent.

Consequently, if you are a woman between the ages of 25 and 44 going on a roller coaster in August, you probably should keep your hands inside the ride. Oh, and take along an Ace bandage.

Mortal Thoughts

He's either dead or my watch has stopped.

—Groucho Marx
Chico, Harpo, Gummo, and Zeppo's brother

Fishing for Fatalities

Fatal Fishing Holes

 Sitting on the creek bank trying to wiggle a dirty worm onto a hook may seem treacherous to some (mostly for the worm, though), but it pales in comparison to the dangers endured by more adventurous anglers. *Outdoor Life* magazine ranked the 6 deadliest fishing spots in the U.S.

1. Columbia Bar. This Oregon site is affectionately known as the "graveyard of the Pacific" by the familiar. During salmon season, boat congestion meets perilous ocean currents to create one hellish fishing environment. In the brief span of a month and a half in 2001, the Coast Guard received 300 distress calls and 13 sailors died.

2. Great Lakes. It's usually the weather on the nearly 95,000-square-mile lakes that causes the most trouble. The Coast Guard performs almost 7,000 rescues each year.

3. Tampa Bay. No, it's not the Buccaneers, but sudden thunderstorms that surprise the 100,000-plus powerboats frequenting the area. Aarrggh, matey!

4. White River. Better hold on to something if the dam's power-generating turbines start up while you're fishing for trout in this Arkansas River. The rate of water flow can increase more than 40 times in a heartbeat.

5. New River. This West Virginia whitewater haven for trophy smallmouth bass racks up a handful of fatalities every year.

6. Hell Canyon/Snake River. Sturgeon larger than an NBA player are the draw; rocks, rapids, and a rollicking current are the danger. Frozen fishsticks, anyone?

Crash and Burn

Rock-n-Roll Deaths, Part I

 In the late '50s, a rock-and-roll show featuring Buddy Holly (with Waylon Jennings on bass), Richie Valens, the Big Bopper, and Dion and the Belmonts was touring the Midwest.

Tired of traveling through Iowa in lousy buses ill-equipped to handle the freezing temperatures, Buddy Holly decided to charter a plane—a single-engine Beechcraft Bonanza. The flu-ridden Big Bopper was a shoo-in for a ride, and Richie Valens tossed a coin with Jennings for the last seat. (Lucky for Jennings that he lost the toss.)

In the early morning of February 3, 1959, the plane took off, despite a snowstorm, and crashed soon afterward. Everyone on board died. Rumor has it that the plane was named *American Pie*. And given the noise kids are making these days, it may very well have been the day the music died.

Want more rockers who died in plane

crashes? How about Otis Redding, Jim Croce (well, a folksinger), Bill Chase (okay, a jazz trumpeter), Ronnie VanZant, Steve Gaines, and Cassie Gaines (all from Lynyrd Skynyrd), Randy Rhodes (while buzzing Ozzy Osborne's tour bus in a plane—capital idea), Stevie Ray Vaughn, Ricky Nelson, and John Denver (not really a rock star, but he played music anyway, right?).

Mortal Thoughts

Life is pleasant. Death is peaceful. It's the transition that's troublesome.

    —Isaac Asimov
Prolific science-fiction author

Die Before You Get Old

Rock-n-Roll Deaths, Part II

So you think more rock stars died in plane crashes than choked on their drug-laced barf? Not so fast, morbid curiosity seeker. In this list tallied by Dial-the-Truth Ministries (no hidden agenda here, we're certain), heart attacks take first prize. The final truth tally:

Heart attack, 42; drug overdose, 40; miscellaneous medical, 37; suicide, 36; auto/cycle crash, 35; cancer, 25; airplane crash, 22; unknown, 21; murdered, 18; alcohol, 9; accident, 6; drowned, 5; brain tumor, 4; AIDS, 4; poisoned, 3; leukemia, 3; electrocuted, 3; stroke, 3; fire 3; choked, 2.

Total Deaths—321.

Expiration Date

Rock-n-Roll Deaths, Part III

Dead at the ripe old age of 27:

1. Dennes Boon of the Minutemen died in a car accident.
2. Kurt Cobain of Nirvana committed suicide.
3. Jimi Hendrix died of a drug overdose (actually the coroner said "inhalation of vomit, due to barbituate intoxication." Lovely.)
4. Robert Johnson (blues singer, but close enough) was poisoned.
5. Brian Jones of The Rolling Stones drowned.
6. Janis Joplin died of a drug overdose.
7. Pigpen of the Grateful Dead died of liver failure (probably a few drinks involved here as well).
8. Jim Morrison of the Doors suffered a heart attack.
9. Al Wilson of Canned Heat chose suicide.

But hey, did you really want to see an old, fat Morrison singing in a Vegas stage show?

Jurassic Rock

Rock-n-Roll Deaths, Part IV

Recently, American gerontologist David Demko investigated the habits of living rock stars and predicted their average life span to be 36.9 years. By those calculations, Rolling Stoner Keith Richards should have died a couple of decades ago.

Mortal Thoughts

I wouldn't mind dying in a plane crash. It'd be a good way to go. I don't want to die in my sleep, or of old age, or OD...I want to feel what it's like. I want to taste it, hear it, smell it. Death is only going to happen to you once; I don't want to miss it.

—Jim Morrison
Rock star and heart-attack victim

Siren Songs

The Most Dangerous Driving Tunes

As if driving weren't dangerous enough, playing some songs in the car can lead to accidents, even death, according to Britain's RAC Foundation for Motoring.

And it's not just that rock-n-roll kids are listening to these days. The most dangerous tune is Richard Wagner's *Ride of the Valkyries*. According to the venerable foundation, it's too loud and its tempo is too fast.

In other words, it gets you too wound up to drive safely.

Music Notes From All Over (the Road)

1. *Ride of the Valkyries* by Richard Wagner
2. *Dies Irae* from Giuseppe Verdi's *Requiem*
3. *Firestarter* by the Prodigy
4. *Red Alert* by Basement Jaxx
5. *Insomnia* by Faithless

War: What Is It
Good For?

War Is Hell

The Deadliest Wars

World War II racked up more than 56.4 million deaths, including more than 405,000 Americans. But for the U.S., the deadliest war was the Civil War.

With more than 368,500 deaths on the Union side and an estimated 258,000 from the Confederate states, more than 626,500 Americans died during the fighting. Of those fatalities, just 204,000 died in battle; disease and privation killed the rest. Gettysburg was the battle with the highest casualty count—23,000 Union soldiers were killed, missing, or wounded, compared with 28,000 Confederates.

Battle Cry

The Highest Battle Body Counts

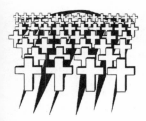 The Battle of Stalingrad, a city with a prewar population of half a million, ended in February 1943 with a total body count of more than 1.1 million—mostly Soviets. Only 1,515 citizens of Stalingrad survived to see the Germans surrender in May 1945.

In World War I, the Battle of the Somme, in which Britain and France fought against Germany (near the Somme River in the north of France) from July 1 to November 19, 1916, resulted in 1.22 million dead and wounded.

Mortal Thoughts
I believe in sex and death—two experiences that come once in a lifetime.

    —Woody Allen
    Author and playwright

The Might to Bear Arms

The Most Dangerous War Ship

If you want to pick a fight with some asshole bully (especially of the Middle Eastern despot variety), get a Nimitz-class aircraft carrier to cover your back.

One of the newest in the U.S. arsenal, the *USS Ronald Reagan*, is 24 stories tall, 1,100 feet long, and carries more than 80 warbirds with a strike range of 1,700 miles. The price tag? A cool $5 billion.

Or, you could have one of those nuclear submarines. It could blow up the entire world.

Mortal Thoughts
We die only once, and for such a long time.

—Moliere
French playwright

40 Bong Hits

Killer Aim

Actually, Major Richard Bong knocked out
40 planes—the most by any American. Major
Bong hailed from southeast Wisconsin, and
the state honored him by naming a large park
in Kansasville the Bong Recreation Area. The
park signs are now mass-produced, and are a
"big hit" at urban teenybopper stores.

Mortal Thoughts

To die will be an awfully big adventure.

—Aristotle
Ancient Greek philosopher

Now That's Firepower

A Million Murderous Shots

Talk about a high rate of fire. Australian Mike O'Dwyer has invented a gun that can fire at a rate of more than 1 million rounds per minute. Compare that with your next-fastest machine gun, which shoots a mere 10,000 rounds per minute.

How does it do it? Instead of spacing the bullets out about 90 feet, like your run-of-the-mill machine gun, the Metal Storm spaces its bullets just a few inches apart.

The 9-mm electronic-trigger weapon comes with a 540-round magazine (even though the 36-barrel prototype can fire about 17,000 rounds per second) and has no moving mechanical parts.

You don't want something like this falling into the wrong hands, so it comes with technology that limits access to the gun's authorized owner. Its inventor adds that it could be loaded with packets of, say plant food, so it could be used to fertilize fields. That's beating swords into plowshares.

Gun Play

The Deadliest Bullet

 There's another situation that guys can think of where size doesn't really matter.

What makes a handgun deadly is not size of the bullet fired, but rather the type of bullet that's in its chamber.

And size for size, the deadliest bullet, says Sgt. Scott Lowenthal, firearms trainer for New York's Metropolitan Transportation Authority police force, is the Black Talon, which has a razor-sharp "claw" that breaks up inside the body, lacerating organs. It's become a dangerous pain-in-the-ass for medical types trying to remove all of the teeny, sharp pieces. "It's supposed to be for law enforcement only, but in America, everything is available for anyone," Lowenthal says.

After the Black Talon comes rounds that explode on impact and Teflon-coated bullets designed to penetrate bulletproof vests.

The Terminator Guy

(One of the) Nastiest Nazis

Hans Rudel was one indestructible Nazi. And he sure liked doing that war thing.

During 4 years of active flying duty, Hans logged 2,530 combat missions in his Junkers JU-87 Stuka dive bomber and destroyed 518-plus tanks, 700 trucks, 150-plus flak and artillery positions, 9 fighters and ground-attack aircraft, hundreds of bridges, railway lines, and bunkers, the Soviet battleship *October Revolution*, the Soviet cruiser *Marat*, and 70 landing craft. He was shot down 32 times, wounded on many occasions—including the partial amputation of his right leg in the spring of 1945, after which he continued to fly with a prosthetic limb.

Oh, yeah, Hans rarely ever went on leave. Hitler even spoke of making him the next Fuhrer, but heck, the Russians rolled into Berlin before that could happen.

It's a Gas

The Deadliest Aerosol Attacks

Chlorine is not just for swimming pools, as World War I combatants could tell you.

First used by the Germans against the French in the 1915 Battle of Ypres, the yellow gas smells like a mixture of pineapple and pepper. It destroys the lungs, thus asphyxiating its victims. Chlorine gas can be neutralized by ammonia, so the armies being gassed distributed masks with pads soaked in urine. They had to be desperate.

Even more effective than chlorine is phosgene, which is more potent in smaller doses. Plus, it kills its victims within 48 hours. Some armies even mixed the two gases together, a concoction they called "white star."

One important note about gas: You can only do it under the right weather conditions. Early in World War I, the British launched a gas attack, but the wind blew it right back into their faces. Not good.

Ban the Bomb

Nuclear Nations

Who really has nuclear weapons? As of spring 2004, here's the total list:

Russia—9,500; United States—9,300; France—460; China—400; Great Britain—185; Israel—between 75 and 130; India—30; Pakistan—15; South Africa—6 (But now maintains that all were dismantled); North Korea—1 to 6.

Now, who's trying like hell to get them (besides al Qaeda)? Saudi Arabia, Iran, Brazil, Argentina and, nervous about North Korea's growing arsenal, Japan.

Okay, so how many nuclear bombs would it take to wipe out everyone on earth? The late, great Dr. Carl Sagan, author and host of *Cosmos* ("Billions and billions..."), calculated that about 100 megatons could produce enough smoke and ash to create a global nuclear winter. That's about 400 bombs.

Pulling No Punches

The Fiercest Fist

The man with the most dangerous punch in recent history would have to be Mas Oyama (1923–1994), a Korean expatriate who lived and trained in Japan and founded the notoriously aggressive Kyokushin karate. "He was famous for killing bulls with his punches," says Robert W. Young, executive editor of *Black Belt* magazine. During the '50s, Oyama fought 52 bulls and killed 3 instantly.

How did he get so strong? "He spent a lot of time training in the mountains and whacking trees," says Young. Those stupid trees probably deserved it.

Hearth, Home, and Headstone

Light My Fire

Hazardous Household Appliances

 Those cheapo halogen lamps, whose bulbs burn at 970 degrees Fahrenheit, have started more than 150 fires and killed 11 people since 1992.

On the bright side, you'll never need a cigarette lighter when you own one of these hot puppies.

And who can forget the early '70s? Nixon was president, the Vietnam War was winding down, and those newfangled microwave ovens could nuke a potato in 4 minutes flat. Trouble was, the earliest models all leaked deadly microwave radiation, giving the newly-liberated American housewife that warm, funny feeling inside.

For a brief, shining moment, the microwave oven earned the rare "not acceptable" rating from that staid guardian of consumerism, the Consumer Reports Testing Center, before saturating the marketplace and becoming as ubiquitous as a TV tuned to ESPN in a bachelor pad. (As a precaution, guys, you may not want to keep them at crotch height.)

Runner-up: Disco-era blow-dryers made with cancer-causing asbestos.

Mortal Thoughts

If my doctor told me I had only 6 minutes to live, I wouldn't brood. I'd type a little faster.

—Isaac Asimov
Overly prolific science fiction writer of more than 500 books

Grill Crazy

The Most Brutal Barbecues

 People also like to use charcoal grills to heat their homes in the winter. Each year, 20 people die from carbon monoxide (CO) poisoning (see page 23) and about 400 hit the emergency room after seeking charcoal's radiant warmth, according to the U.S. Consumer Product Safety Commission.

Mortal Thoughts

Death is not the end. There remains the litigation over the estate.

—Ambrose Bierce
American humorist, missing in Mexico since 1913

Step Lively (or Deadly)

The Deadliest Place in the House

Falls in the home account for about 5.6 million injuries each year, according to the Home Safety Council, a nonprofit organization dedicated to preventing unintentional injuries in the household. Seventeen percent of all fall deaths were associated with stairs or steps.

Mortal Thoughts

Take death, for example. A great deal of our effort goes into avoiding it. We make extraordinary efforts to delay it, and indeed often consider its intrusion a tragic event. Yet we would find it hard to live without it. Death gives meaning to our lives. It gives importance and value to time. Time would become meaningless if there were too much of it. If death were indefinitely put off, the human psyche would end up, well, like the gambler in The Twilight Zone *episode.*

—Ray Kurzweil
Inventor and all-around really smart guy

171

Maimed in Toyland

Treacherous Toys

The U.S. Consumer Product Safety Commission estimates that toy-related injuries for children happen at a rate of about 150,000 per year.

Almost half (46 percent) of these injuries occurred to children under the age of 5. The face leads the way as the body part that sustained the most injuries—37,800—with the head coming in at a distant second at 22,100.

And it isn't just the little boys either. Girls make up 40 percent of the total.

Toy-related deaths for the decade of the '90s, compiled by the U.S. Public Interest Research Group from CPSC data, indicate balloons to be enemy number one for kids.

In fact, the CPSC is so concerned about the suffocation threat of balloons that they advise no one under 8 years old be allowed to play with a balloon unattended.

In the past 30 years, more than 100 children have died of suffocation with a toy balloon—over 50 in the '90s alone. Choking by small balls, marbles, toys, or toy parts make up the balance of the choking deaths that represent more than 60 percent of all toy-related deaths for the past 10 years.

Tricycle and riding-toy accidents comprise almost 20 percent of the decade's fatalities, with the balance being a combination of strangulation, death by toy chest (for 75 years—until 1987—the Lane Company built about 12 million cedar chests that automatically locked when the lid closed. Kids would trap themselves in the chest and suffocate.), and other incidents.

And all of that is before they get strapped into one of those recalled car seats. Hey, maybe the TV is not so bad after all.

The Roof Is on Fire

Candle Casualties

Almost 7,000 house fires are started every year by candles, according to the U.S. Consumer Product Safety Commission.

Annually, the fiery torches cause about 700 injuries and nearly 100 deaths. Well over half of these fires are the result of leaving a burning candle unsupervised. Only a tenth of these are started by children playing with lit candles. Most kids know you've got to blow them all out to get your wish.

Mortal Thoughts
A single death is a tragedy; a million deaths is a statistic.

—Joseph Stalin
Famous despot

Fatal Fashions

Deadly Drawstrings

 Consider the lowly drawstring. Since 1985, there have been 17 deaths and 42 injuries attributed to drawstrings. More than half of the entanglements occurred on playground slides. And then there were buses, cribs, escalators, fences, farm equipment, turn signal levers, ski lifts, and tricycles. Now, however, it's illegal to put drawstrings in children's clothing.

Mortal Thoughts
When you've told someone that you've left them a legacy, the only decent thing to do is to die at once.

—Samuel Butler
Author of *The Way of All Flesh*

Helmet Hair

The Most Hazardous Hobby

Years ago, the only bicyclists who wore helmets were in the Tour de France. Today, the U.S. Consumer Product Safety Commission reports that half of all riders in America do.

Ironically, more children under the age of 16 (69 percent) regularly wear helmets than do adults (38 percent), even after imploring little Johnny to keep his on regardless of the heat. So it shouldn't be a surprise that more adults die (700 per year) than kids (200 per year) on bikes. And those grown-ups probably can't even do a wheelie.

Mortal Thoughts
I am become Death, shatterer of worlds.

—J. Robert Oppenheimer, upon witnessing the explosion of the first atomic bomb. Physicist credited for causing the entire human race to live in fear of total annihilation for the last 60 years.

Practical Bad Joke

A Perilous Practical Joke

 While hosting a party, a fellow in New Jersey thought it would be a great practical joke to pack a muzzle-loader rifle with cigarette butts and shoot his roommate in the chest. (Another great idea spawned by a man emboldened by alcohol.)

He was too good of a shot; a couple of the butts penetrated the roommate's rib cage just below his heart and killed him. Add the aggravated manslaughter charge to the 2 counts of aggravated assault from different incidents at the party, and you get one crummy host. Didn't anybody tell this guy that cigarettes are deadly?

Bad Air Days

Smoggy Suffocation

Ever since we started burning things to keep warm, the air has been getting dirty.

The Romans were bothered by the mess of oil and wood. The Industrial Revolution threw more fuel on the fire. Thermal inversion, a situation where a higher layer of warmer air traps cooler air at lower altitudes, tends to keep polluted air close to the ground.

Thermal inversion proved deadly in 1930, when 60 people died and thousands became ill in a low-lying river valley in Belgium. Just 18 years later, 20 people died in Donora, Pennsylvania, and thousands were sent to hospitals as a result of some tremendously polluted air that hung around for days. Almost half of the inhabitants developed respiratory problems. The resulting investigation of the Donora disaster is credited with initiating clean air legislation in the U.S.

But an even worse disaster occurred in England. London fog is hardly a new concept; the city is close to cool water and air, and that's how fog is born. Even smog is nothing new: Locals started burning coal in the 1600's, and the smoke mixed with fog (ergo, smog).

On December 4, 1952, however, a black fog enveloped London, dropping visibility to less than 10 feet. As a result, the city simply shut down. The airports closed and people abandoned their cars in the street. A performance of *La Traviata* was canceled due to the smog in the theater. In fact, all movies were canceled. By December 7, visibility was down to 1 foot in yellow fog.

When the heavy smog lifted, 4 days after it began, more than 4,000 Londoners were dead due to cardiac arrest and respiratory illness. The incident was blamed on excessive coal burning, and shortly thereafter, laws were enacted to phase out coal for clean-burning natural gas.

The Stuff We Couldn't Categorize

Cursed Object

The Most Jinxed Jewel

Supposing you buy into the whole curse thing—it's easier than taking responsibility for your actions—then the deadliest curse would be the badly misnamed Hope Diamond.

The French gem merchant who sold it to Louis XIV was ripped apart by dogs. Louis died of some disease—maybe smallpox, maybe gangrene. Marie Antoinette wore it and lost her head in the French revolution.

American buyer Evalyn McLean had the diamond blessed in a church, but, even then, her 9-year-old son was struck by a car while carrying the gem in his pocket, her mom died of pneumonia, and her daughter overdosed on sleeping pills. Both wore the diamond.

After McLean, herself, finally expired, jeweler Harry Winston bought the Hope Diamond and donated it to the Smithsonian Institution in 1958. With America as its owner, we've had Vietnam, Watergate, President Richard Nixon, 9/11, and Gulf War II. Let's get rid of it before any more Bushes get elected.

Not a Very Good Year

The Deadliest Years in History

 2003 was a brutal year nature-wise; roughly 60,000 people died from earthquakes, typhoons, storms, wildfires, and other disasters.

Topping the list was the 40,000 deaths in Bam, Iran, following an earthquake.

The worst year (Swiss Re, a global insurance company, has been keeping track) was 1970, when storms and resulting floods killed 300,000 in Bangladesh, and a Peruvian earthquake killed 60,000.

The 2003 total was the 7th highest on Swiss Re's list. As for 2003's worst manmade disaster—the sinking of a Bangladeshi ferry that killed 528 people.

Dead-Man's Hand

The Most Dangerous Card Game

When Jack McCall plugged card-shark Wild Bill Hickock in the back while he was playing poker in the Mann-Lewis Saloon, in Deadwood, South Dakota, the gambling gun-slinger held two pair—black aces and black 8s.

To this day, no one can agree on the 5th card. Deadwood has a 5 of diamonds on display, while first-hand accounts say it was a jack of diamonds. According to the transcripts of McCall's trial, it was a 9 of diamonds. A Ripley's Believe it or Not museum displays a queen of clubs, and in the 1936 movie *The Plainsman*, Gary Cooper, as Wild Bill, holds a king of spades.

Death List

Not Quite So Deadly

According to the World Heath Organization, things are getting better...really. Here are the worldwide figures.

Child Mortality per 1000 Live Births
147 in 1970; 80 in 2002

Child Deaths (under the age of 5)
17 million in 1970; 10.5 million in 2002

Average Life Expectancy at Birth
46.5 years in 1950; 65.2 years in 2002

Mortal Thoughts
I don't mind dying, the trouble is you feel so bloody stiff the next day.

—George Axlerod
Screenwriter

Not a Sign of Freedom

The Most Hostile Flag

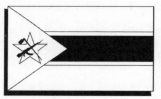 The least friendly flag has to be Mozambique's (see pages 78 and 79), where instead of stars and stripes, the flag has a drawing of an M-16 machine gun. That's nature's way of saying, "do not touch."

Mortal Thoughts
The trouble with heart disease is that the first symptom is often hard to deal with—sudden death.

   —Michael Phelps, MD
   Cardiologist

Part It Out

Creepy Cremation

An owner of a crematorium in southeast Los Angeles had a clever idea.

In 2000 and 2001, he made almost $500,000 selling off parts from several bodies to medical researchers. He removed various parts prior to cremation—including heads and spines—and sold them under the name Biotech Anatomical. After pleading guilty in late 2003 to more 60 counts of grave mutilation and embezzlement, he drew the maximum penalty of 20 years in prison.

Mortal Thoughts
It costs me never a stab nor squirm
To tread by chance upon a worm.
"Aha, my little dear," I say,
"Your clan will pay me back one day."

—Dorothy Parker
Celebrated wit and member of the
Algonquin Hotel's famous Round Table.

No Man's Land

The Deadliest Planet

500 000 000 Who hasn't been in a situation that seemed to last forever—a math class, a lunch date, or just watching water boil?

But really, that's just an illusion; nothing lasts forever—not even the human race.

So, how long until the end of humanity? This is the type of question usually addressed by people wearing thick glasses and long white coats while looking through large telescopes. University of Washington astrobiologists say that we are already on the downhill side of life on ol' planet earth.

Don't panic however, they figure we have about 500 million years before the sun gets so hot that all plant and animal life (that includes us, of course) will disappear. That is assuming, of course, that some idiotic despot or wild-eyed terrorist doesn't blow the darn thing up before then.

The astrobiologists liken the end of the world to evolution in reverse. Animal and plant life will retreat to water for survival, resulting in a period much like the beginning of the planet. Then microbes will dominate, though they will eventually cook as well.

They note the mere presence of Earth in the vast solar system with all of its water and life is our incredible good fortune. But, ultimately, we will all go away for good. Hey, it was a great ride for a billion or so years. In the meantime, take care of your nest, dig the planet, and above all, enjoy yourself.

That's All Folks

The Deadliest Thing of All...Death

How many people have died, ever?

In 1995, Carl Haub, a demographer for the Population Reference Bureau, published a hypothesis of the number of people alive today as a percentage of the total number of people that have ever lived, based on demographic observations. He postulates that the average life span was a paltry 10 years for the preponderance of human existence. Now that's babies having babies.

Projecting the birth and death rate and allowing for events like the Bubonic Plague, Haub estimates that 5.5 percent of all people who have ever lived are still alive. If we use an estimate of the current world population at say, 6.42 billion, Haub concludes that 100 percent of the people who have ever lived is about 116.7 billion.

Nathan Keyfitz, Harvard professor and

statistician for more than 30 years, was one of the first to greatly complicate the study of population by combining it with computers and complex higher mathematics. He did an early calculation of the number of people that have ever lived starting 1 million years ago with a pair of homo sapiens ancestors.

In 1999, at the request of University of Hawaii political science professor Glen Paige, for his book *Nonkilling Global Political Science,* U of H mathematics professor Tom Ramsey updated Keyfitz's study.

This is the kind of math that makes your head hurt. He systematically arrives at an answer of 96.1 billion. These 2 estimates of the number of people who have ever lived differ by about 20 billion. Average the 2 and you get 106 billion. Subtract the 6.42 billion still alive and the answer is: about 100 billion people have died since time began.

The End of the World

Earth's Extinction

 So, once all life is gone, then what?

Well, after life ends in 500 million years, those same fellows from the University of Washington (see page 188) hypothesize that the sun will continue to expand, becoming a red giant, and the earth will essentially vaporize. That is, after it cooks Mercury and Venus. But this should take another 7 billion years.

Really going to miss this place.

Mortal Thoughts
You can live to be a hundred if you give up all the things that make you want to live to be a hundred.

—Woody Allen
Former boyfriend of actress Mia Farrow